City Flowers, filaments
and Arches,

Shadows,

City Flowers, filaments and Arches,

Shadows,

Poetry

SY HAKIM

iUniverse, Inc.
New York   Bloomington

City Flowers, filaments and Arches,Shadows, Poetry

iUniverse books may be ordered through booksellers or by contacting:

iUniverse
1663 Liberty Drive
Bloomington, IN 47403
www.iuniverse.com
1-800-Authors (1-800-288-4677)

Because of the dynamic nature of the Internet, any Web addresses or
links contained in this book may have changed since publication and
may no longer be valid. The views expressed in this work are solely those
of the author and do not necessarily reflect the views of the publisher,
and the publisher hereby disclaims any responsibility for them.

ISBN: 978-1-4502-5338-3 (sc)
ISBN: 978-1-4502-5339-0 (ebook)

Printed in the United States of America

iUniverse rev. date: 9/1/2010

Index

City Flowers

City flowers, grown, uncut
roses and vibrating colors –
reds and brilliant yellows,
upward exuberance thrust
amidst green stalks and thorns:
flung between the buttresses,
the building's ruins
and brick remains
a boy's joy, contagious
beyond the low wall.
There was a building, here
collapsed, now a "lot"
an almost empty spare space,
big city abandoned,
flat and sprinkled dirt
scattered with pebbles and stones,
detritus – remnants –
with dark dank dirt mixed:
beneath red sun and motif,
motives of Spring
among ruins of collapse,
hopes amidst relapse –
a boy, arms raised laughter
and vibrant roses grown.

Before The Bridge

Before the bridge,
crossing
amber time, held
preserved, perceived
blinking caution – pause:
waiting at the bridge
imponderable memories,
life as memories – paused;
life as the utilization,
choices crossing;
bridge, gap
time, delay;
choice is the utilization,
fruitilization,
sum of the accidental.

Within memories' choices
pause, stop, select,
step, go:
hesitating step,
go, stop, pause – go
with the blinking amber;
lights slide into motion,
commotion of lights – glide –
alternating with steps,
hesitating – echoes –
time gap
beneath tower base
and rising steel,
curving
cables and silent emotion…

Memories glide, slide,
a hesitation,
a visitation-
bridge gap
a time delay;
start with a stutter-step:
initiate a control,
colors – spinning
beyond control – cascading
life as memories' choices –
no choice –
before the bridge,
alternating before, between
blinking choices and lights
and amber warnings.

Waiting, stopped, go,
pause, stop, - select:
disseminate?
discriminate?
there is no choice
but choices;
time play
time delay
life is the living
memories going, giving
and the accidental;
start the motion – emotion –
take the step
stutter step
stutter…and…step.

Incubi

From the incubi
self risen through thoughts:
culled sleepless dreams
rise white spirits,
sylph-en forms,
and the wordless tunes
of songs
rarely heard,
more rarely sung...
forbidden hints of tunes
and fairytales of desires'
whisper, seemingly white-
transparent
wisps of haze
drift- a glowing glaze
across the demi- obscure:
ephemeral covers
and bands of colors
wrung,
floated down
with falling rainbows:
formless forms
converging
guiltless, suggestive
beguiling memories...
a soft indeterminate
between known and unknown
moonrise and sunset,
confusions
or self doubts,
silver slivers or gold:

unrequited desires
form the mold,
the release and hold
of the symbiotic call,
the slow fall
into undetermined nightmare:
incubus
between damnation and desire....

Imponderable Memories

Imponderable memories
arching,
the bridge,
ecstatic thoughts,
erotic,
irrevocable:
barely perceptible,
memories haunt
undefined;
ethereal weight –
conscience
and consciousness –
a Mona Lisa's smile
of fragile self
barely remembering act
or consequence.

Subdued self standing
poised before the bridge –
and pause;
entrance way and exit
to past and to beyond;
thought flecks, flickerings,
contradictions
and possibilities:
steel towers rising
and sky-thrust cables
light as air,
blue flecked
and light flashed
arched and curved –

a beginning,
the ephemeral way...

Imponderable memories
and the bridge,
blinking lights and time,
line reflections,
possibility and halt:
stop or go
cross or pause,
transitory
car lights and bridge lights,
pass-ways across the waters,
search-way to the winds,
ecstatic blowing winds,
cross winds,
and touched, felt
transient discoveries
of the mind.

Irretrievable acts,
grasped at memories,
vague thoughts,
white floating
unreachable flecks;
dissipating light:
the pause haunts;
the stop before start
or the return,
the ethereal absence
and vague stretch
touching at fingertips;
the bridge,
imponderable, arching
irrevocable memories.

The Brother

I

Haunted, trapped in distorted memory,
proposals, non-premeditated lies –
by eugenics, dark and light,
brown and blond, lost, found –
hunted, the eldest brother, confused,
confirmed in the myth of tradition,
the brother writhes under the twisted truth,
ties the lies, the failed attempts, intents
until he can neither instruct or protect:
intense, instincts confused
he is that he is,
outdated gestures are rendered useless,
his inept attempts to again protect,
to assure a younger – heart;
to secure, to assuage, to calm,
to seal a simmering wound,
to heal the unmerited hurt:
there is no longer the feel,
a reach; his once sure touch
to make better a scraped knee
or a youthful wounded psyche – gone:
the oldest brother, again, failed!

II

Self, failed:
frustration is the non- achieved;
guilt is built within the family,
duress inhaled in a stultifying air,
built into along with the care,
the hereditary genetics
the synapses, eugenic connectors,
the growth of sibling attentiveness –
the structure and rivalry:
frustration self confounded,
family impounded, formed
and formed the eldest brother,
the obligations, mentality of concern,
growth grown sense of debilitated self,
dependent worth – independent obligations;
weighted guilt that time develops,
distorts, starts and restarts,
a whirl of world,
relation ships unsettled and faltering dreams,
his trial of the frail fumbling family's schemes,
crumbling relationships, trails,
goals wished and lost – abandoned;
the slow decay of the every day,
of hurt and hope derailed,
living dreams, ambitions impaled,
of the host of fallen hopes,
brothers and sisters – love –
crumbled times every day, evaporating,
promised possibilities failed.

III

Two sisters, one gone, one failing:
first into the darkness, Eleanor
the creative, depth plumbing critic,
gone, alone at night,
subject to a darkening time –
no sunrise! –
Eleanor and thought – a superior tension,
cigarettes and black coffee:
brain or heart, hemorrhage –
life fright strikes, alone:
a call, the long distance-telephone –
and nothing a brother – too late –
an older brother can do:
gone the plumbing mind,
the inquisitive searching,
the open determined brown eyes,
and no ability, too late to offer,
to have made her life…more…
Now, years later, Eleanor
still tailings of her memory,
her written words, works
in sites and inquiries, hurt, haunt:
ingenious in sites, trapped,
trailings and words,
concepts typed – and fled;
relationships failed,
guilt still, not abandoned:
Eleanor…dead…

IV

There was a brother,
the younger, youngest of four,
Victor who was
appearance diminished – wasn't:
a slow growing schizophrenic –
manic – depressive classic by twenty two;
suspicians and achievements,
lows hidden beneath captivating looks,
the beguiling of a misleading smile:
Victor, handsome with accomplishments,
a lawyer, passed the bar, at twenty one –
and then twenty two, unknowingly, done;
the slow downward unravel,
the manic-depressive spiral to done,
Victor Philip, parent named,
historic names flagged from success,
histrionic younger brother
separated by expectations and years:
here too no farewell
no final personal tears – good by –
rather a slow noticed disappearance
into the developing disease – lost,
a mere shadow in a shadowed world
haunting a foreign place –
London? – alone,
disappeared into self –
"I need a brother"
telephoned – alone – trapped, lost…

V

Neither memories – nor words – can confront
the realities of diagnosis,
comfort childhood mistaken hypnosis,
confront the too fast craft of time,
nurtured heredity or genetics:
neither forgiveness nor grace,
the magic disappears,
hurt is not displaced,
no longer assuaged by tears;
passing time finds, rediscovery, and diminishes
disillusions of the elder,
the older "big brother";
illusions evaporated into the dark
of disappearance,
the far away, the receding
of the world's words:
memories electric impulses still travel,
traversing, trailing shocked traces
from the hung up telephone…

VI

Time and age –
Shakespeare's stage – reflective
and now a slow and continual dawning,
or settling, the absolute warning;
the ultimate prognosis was "genetics
and hereditary" – neurothopy:
another long distance call,
Gami, Gamelia, Gloria the younger,
a sister who would have been
boarding on the stage, acclaimed,
talented youthful promises of fame
short-cut, cut short –
the expression, the exception
of our mother's fear,
outdated confusing of actress and prostitute
without a recognition
of a daughter's talent or worth;
[a mother, daughter of her past,
pulled from school –
9 years of A's
to work in Woolworth's 5 and dime]
and now a mother's misplaced domination,
a wife quieted father
and he, the older brother, away,
and the sister's talent squashed,
sub-merged by a mother's determination;
Gami called from San Diego –
that perfect climate
of too perfect a place –
and once again wires to trace
that cross a continent, and space:

there is no immunity from time
or heredity or memory,
we image our aging face
in our bathroom mirrors,
reflecting what has been lost,
mis-placed,
with only the lingering trace
of frustration, disappointment
and the prescribed pills
too neatly arranged in place...
Where is the apology,
the remnants of lost,
the sorcerers' magic –
big brother's solutions
the once childish power to heal,
to assuage the hurts...
all becomes darkness, diminishes,
memories lost with the weight of age –
the big brother's vacuous "I'm sorry"
his prancing about his insubstantial stage:
all lights dim, all dreams transcend,
all space declines to its darkening, permanent end.

Multiplicating Memories

The carved stone, sculpture, centered
in the Veneto square:
entrance sign of the elephant,
curved ivory tusk beneath the arch
shadowed walkway, red-rimmed
with the entering sun:
yellow-white, Dante in full light,
pensive, standing, gazing, warning
between the past – the Scaligere –
and the future: tombs, meditation;
Dante's statue recalling memories...

Between the columned palace
and the medieval tower
on the still quiet square –
set – the silent ever-present statue
more resilient than the noise
entering from the market – Piazza Erbe –
where people jostle and mingle:
Dante, dominating beyond the archway.

Dante and Dante's shadow,
multiplicating memories,
recalling, reworking history,
projecting through passing time
and the personal stories
of those long gone – youth vanquished –
and the jostling mingling crowds;
Dante silently dominating, converging
multiplicating memories and applications,
prior events and supplications

through pursed stone lips;
Dante seeing, visualizing, recalling
the rise and the fall
and the possible prayers of application,
guided reconciliation…but loss:
Dante dedicating memories and prophesies;
red-rimmed time fore warned
predicate the fore told probabilities.

Dante's statue, standing – defiant –
dominating the sun filled Veneto square,
meditating; if slowly disintegrating yet prognosticating
under the vernal Verona sun:
Beatrice was – is – youth unfulfilled,
Florentine memories of innocence and beauty,
brilliance, beatitude light filled memories recalled
and probabilities denied – vanished:
carved stone and memories slowly disintegrating,
there is no possibility, no returning, retrieving,
no re-working ever-fading time.

I too have stood in Dante's shadow
in the yellow-white light filled square,
sat at the foot, the pedestal – the promise
of the pensive – relentless – statue
and worried over multiplicating memories,
actions undone: replicating hopes,
multiplicating thoughts, gratitudes and fortitudes –
futures limited, fading beneath an ever lengthening shade…

The slowly eroding statue still stands,
lips pursed, a silent recalling – foretelling,
a dimming memory of once sought sunlight,
of a white incomprehensible,
a permissible ethereal beyond brilliance:

now, a dimming memory of the blinding light
diminished, obliterates want and desire – all…
The statue's shadow prognosticates,
recalling the failure of youth,
the darkness of feeble attempts,
of tentative moments paused, passed
beyond possibilities once yearned for:
Dante fore tells with warnings of loss,
recalls Beatrice's disappeared promise,
Virgil's limits, the incomprehensible yearning
and the determined turning;
a still more silent, more profound aspect falls:
an eternity of absolute – black.

Children play across the square –
school is out: yellow images and red,
tourists wander in and about
and Dante – the pensive statue – still stands,
silent desire unfilled, a slow decay
harboring more-dire warnings:
run! The sun will never-the-less set – red!
The shadows always lengthen – slow onslaught –
obscuring even the statue, the square
and damning Virgil's lingering songs;
Beatrice's beauty will fade,
to remain only a vague symbol, barely recalled
of a youth dissipated, dissolved, disappeared:
moments passing and multiplicating
are memories feared to fade, mere shadows,
notes obscuring into absolute loss…
Only the dense blackness of time – reverberating.

Beyond Color

Bright light
white light
colors fragment
the once still night –
Sparkles
Illuminate the dark:

Art as creation,
art as color:
beyond dark space,
vacume black and silence,
unmoving strings, silent,
unmarked, un-plucked space-
a gentle quick touch,
inspiration and mystery-
an awakening
an impact of vibration
between silence and dark,
the touch erases "stark":
interplay equals motion,
plucked strings test,
vibrate, form and design,
structure and line,
a resultant rhythm,
beat, the contrast of rest:
movement becomes motion,
the paradox of still
creates creation best.

Caused vibrations gently caressed
creates a contrast,
a coming and becoming-
a finite-
the awareness of being:
the contacts create contrasts,
linked, mystical-"luck"-
internal and external,
eternal vibrations,
visions of being becoming
the magical thing-Color itself

White becoming,
being forming
light born from mystery
of touch...
"Let there be light..."
the special spark
creates contrasts,
white illums the dark,
cancels the dull void,
the negative naught:
explosions of sparks
vibrating visions
luminescence, essence
no longer caught
between dark
and the rainbow arch;
the arc curves the motion
blinding white, pure,
explodes in foliation of color:
sparkles sparkle
across a universe of mind:
color is, color becomes
an evident of rhythm,

of creations' strings,
an oscillating find
vibrating, ringing,
differentiating and defining,
a final completing touch,
the accent,
the emphasis of the singular,
the identity of being,
created, evident...

Bright light
white light
all encompassing light-
sparkles illuminate the dark,
colors shatter the night:

Beyond color is color
is
the symbol sigh,
the simple exacting:
the subtlety and emphasis
extracting the final defining:
the mysterious touch creating
the uniqueness,
a creation
of color binding identity...
Beyond color is
Color
Is ...

Beneath the Arches

Beneath, in the shadow
below the high arch,
the sandstone curve,
amidst the mist
of the desert
and before the winds
storm the cactus,
the ancient stones are:
a tenuous approach
acknowledges the presence
the essence –
memories retracing repetitions,
visions of past,
incantations
repeating across ancient time...

Two figures bend,
gentle silent reflections blend,
clouds and fogs forms;
genuflections,
before the bent knee
windblown distances end:
thoughts search,
reach for the trend beyond,
the spirits portend;
sand not yet sand,
impervious, impermanence,
silent set songs, evaporating
prayers seeking,
mist with echoes,
shadows search the sky...

The seen, the imagined,
visions absorb the desert,
climbing clouds, illusions
amidst a flood of mirages –
desert flowers, windblown
sand of ancient arid rocks
swallow suggestive memories:
mirrors of times to come,
departed spirits songs
reflect and are sung –
thoughts hung on vapors of air,
ethereal images,
ochre-white clouds
and twisting dirt devils;
remembrances without answers…

Bridges, Arches and Melting Snow

Bridges, arches and boulders,
sandstone, shale and granite,
remnants fallen: melting snow and reticent memories
pressed, passed winters' recollections
of those who walked here, hunted,
haunted the cliff-side caverns –
precarious cliff-stone foot holds and caves,
precious footprints over time, a passing ago…
time imprinted, carved deep into the grey gorge,
weather blown, wind arched, water bridged,
broken arches and curved grey passages,
white snow fields and melting water runs,
ruins decaying, erosion tracing cuts
into the diminishing plateau.

Elements and artifacts, remainders and memories
described; inscribed petroglyphs on free standing stone,
lone brown buttes and red/grey Needles,
footprints, and beyond, carving project thoughts
into another conscience, a consciousness, a call:
scattering shale, granite boulders break beneath melting snow,
you too and your vision will ultimately fall,
bypassed, absorbed into the relentless, insistent flow…

Slow Emergence

A slow emergence,
the body
slithers the self-
slow-
from the shadows,
obscuring ,
un-winding.
uncoiling
from smoothly brightening colors,
stretching
from the once
murky would be
of colorless self;
no bright breezy flags
welcoming
waving with the wind,
but a quiet
and a quasi sensuous self,
slowly drawn, withdrawn
fills in,
emerging from time and contradiction,
from self and erase;
the internal contest,
external conquest:
mind tending body,
body re-inventing mind-
ever the contest
to the final toss-
the retrospect:
a slow emergence
to self,
the impending
the final loss....

From The Castle

From the castle
youth as green as growth
and gentle future-
a promise of inevitability-
it shall become and be-
problems ever unraveled,
with triumphs
and beguiling smiles;
gentle unworried youth
with light steps and dances,
with leaps and bounds
and courtesies beguiling-
promises to be   traveled
on verdant paths
toward rainbows;
youth is the promise
and the factor-
customs and costumes,
a brilliance of colors and self,
beauty and assurances
reflecting as shards of glass,
brilliance and form glittering,
flickering in the ever sunlight:
Youth Is green and growth
and tomorrows visions-
a romantic castle to come,
paths amidst full leafed trees,
a soft flowing blue-green river:
Green is a song
sung amidst the garden flowers,
the gentle growing grasses,

the soft gentle breaths of Ophelia:
the green leaves do not fall
in the Springtime,
or upon Ophelia,
flower covered youth
idly floating;
Ophelia ,from the castle,
floating down the blue-green
the timeless countryside,
the unconcerned river...

Stasis

There is no summer!
No stasis,
no stability, no longer seasons:
all is going up – or down;
Springtime becomes Autumn's cousin
As Autumn is Winter's;
Summer would have a stop –
a fulfillment fulfilled and fulfilling,
an ever blooming maturity,
a fullness of self
proscribed
without the admission of motion,
of the going down…
Winter is the past of Summer
made permanent,
the residue, the deposit of time,
the end of past motion:
the ridicule of self.

Terminal

Star struck, infatuated youth
unanswered,
generations unasked, unrealized:
would it have mattered,
made a difference,
when I had married –first-
once, generations, scores ago?
Tattered youth doesn't know,
only hypothesis and hopes
without understanding,
implications too easily misread:
the destination is the going,
the stop is involuntary,
validating or not...
unforeseen, unnoticed, the bump
in the hill,
the hump of diversion,
the divergence,
bend, break of the road,
the parting and the stop,
the division of intent,
self interest
and the ambulatory of way...
Youth can never be correct
or answered:
to go is not to know
where the splitting starts
or the going ends.

Unfiltered

The hunger still hurts:
the thirst
resists the colored shadow
of the setting sun;
classical music strains
to enter autumn windows,
a distorting kaleidoscope:
is it springtime already,
already early after the damp
and the snow have fallen,
another mosaic
reflecting external time?
But there are no roses,
no design of daffodils
or bright Springtime birds
chittering, flittering
across the outside
still open windows:
music and recorded applause
drift with the rifts of motors;
better the music even without the muse
than the autos:
yearning transports all
across place
to the undiminished isolation
of individual, engulfing space.

Beyond Color

Bright light
white light
colors fragment
the once still night-
Sparkles
illuminate the dark:

Art as creation
art as color:
beyond dark space,
vacuum black and silence,
unmoving strings, silent,
unmarked, un-plucked space-
a gentle quick touch,
inspiration and mystery-
an awakening
an impact of vibration
between silence and dark,
the touch erases "stark":
interplay equals motion,
plucked strings test,
vibrate, form and design,
structure and line,
a resultant rhythm,
beat, the contrast of rest:
movement becomes motion,
the paradox of still
creates creation best.

Bright light
white light
all encompassing light-
sparkles illuminate the dark,
colors shatter the night:
beyond is
the symbol,
the simple exacting;
the subtlety and emphasis
extracting the final defining:
the mysterious touch
creating
uniqueness:

Beyond Color Is ...

The Painting

The frame is the final fitting,
the completing black, the boundary,
the border which secures and separates
the act and the intent:
Measured to an exactness
here-to–fore never attempted –
nor achieved –
it holds, it binds the deepest,
the disparate parts
with which we content our lives –
an inaccurate art
we would bend to our will;
but still… art is an evolving construct,
a composite, a utilization
of the accidental…
Call the bindery, give the measurements,
order the frame – in black –
for color lacks, has no finality:
thus, once bound, there is no re-taking,
no retracing –
the painting becomes, is   what it was.

Exhibition

I hang myself to remember
or un-remember, to die
each time I frame sung pictures
or words: black matt rectangles
and self splayed against the wall;
colors and forms distract
yet the whole self blanches,
bleaches under the onslaught,
the arrival of the uncaring unknown;
groups crowd an unrecognized self,
a universe of staring strangers
dissolving images duly reflected,
refracted in a purple wine glass:
awareness and thought are lost
beyond, on the other side of the wall...

Echo laughter and selves assemble,
vacuous talk, to dissemble,
self abnegation, suicide without murder:
the uninstructed, unstructured, unrestricted, glide –
the slide – unrecognized –
caught in the strangers distracted laughter:
the dark juice, distilled purple
mortality, immortality,
the darkness of the universe,
the blackness of dark matter;
a gasp, an involuntary grasp
searches after the matter, the absolute
self/non-self on exhibition: hung
matt black rectangle... framed.

The Blue Window

Blue and born from blue-
prussian and cobalt
cerulean and marine-
blue colors shade a palette,
pitched and thrown,
jagged shards,
streaks against a sky:
dark night's dim light-
reflected light-
fading blue-white,
declining moon –waning
blue shades in a patched sky:
streaks and stretches
refracted and reflected ,
streaks of tears
blue as the color of memory,
the time marker,
delineator of disintegrating shades,
records-the fading of memory…

Impressions: Expressions:
the window-
I have been here
before this tattered night,
before the fading moon,
encircled blue-white moon,
declining, red rimmed,
held passage,
deflected waning passage:
I, before the reflected moon,
cut, quarter cut visions,

white fictions
and encircled bodies,
full bodies,
impetuous
youth's reflections
unbridled passions
and flicks of flesh tone-
impermenance
amidst deepest blue.

I had been there:
full passion
cresting moon
with tentative scratches
of tinted clouds,
soft heard music tones...
where?
Somewhere
there are the stars
passions and celestial bodies
barely recorded- recalled-
white with youth
browned with sun,
wood cut
and crops planted,
flowering trees, reproduced
across the more blue heavens-
youth filled bodies
in bedrooms darkened
below the fleeting night...

Hold time:
time held -yesterday-
today's permanent blue tomorrow-
sunset refracted

moonrise is all:
bodies held
and time fled,
caressed, scratched,
stretched across an impassioned sky-
midnight hue sky-
permanent blue
where youth easily enters:
Time leaves with the dawn,
a story fore-cast
into tomorrow
and fore told:
full encircled decadent moon
waning moon, descendent
into the night-blue sky.

Blue night ,colors,
shades and shards
thrown against the night,
the white held
fragile, fading memories:
passions fuel
full gentle bodies:
young trembling
anxious smooth bodies,
youth !
and temptation born;
a caress
fleets even tomorrow
past memories
into impressions,
unsure expressions,
unkempt, hazy,
marked and jagged
scratches on a window pane,

before, beyond,
beneath the darkening moon...

I have been there-
here
before the window
in the fading blue night ;
I saw her—you
yesterday
before the window
wrapped in colors of blue
shades of light;
just yesterday-
tomorrow...
Today the glass cracked:
images,impressions ,
hazed facts
all shattered:
unmuffled, the slivers fall
blue-white from a patched sky,
shards of memory
disintegrate, silent

on the resiliant, accepting grass...

Magenta Sun

Static disc
unmoved
dark red sun
and the flowing of flooding time;
rivulets,
a rushing river
turbulence
disjointing thought and place:
red sun, imbalance
unbalanced memories
cascading white clouds,
semblances of suggestion
reflection
partial recollection;
special forms
hint special spirits,
spun cloud drifts
building
partial imprints
from unremembered time...

Dark red sun,
magenta disc-
uninvolved-
deep dark overseeing
a touch to paused,
passed suggested,
and present,
fixed above
white water percolating
white clouds accumulating

and white frothed time;
white water broiling
white clouds roiling
insinuations,
intrusions warping delusions,
dissolving illusions,
pictures' memories
unresolved...

Time
crosses the footbridge
haltingly,
connections
tentatively serve
severed memories
and weakening desire:
red dark disc,
magenta sun,
watching
the turbulent flow
of dissembled
ending time.

The Quiet Poet

[When any everything is Art,
Aesthetics is...not]

    The artist-poet, hunched, quiet,
    sits in his reflective corner:
    what has been done
    needs not be redone;
    paintings and statues,
    sculpture forms and images,
    design molds and colors, cascading –
    the brightness blinds the dulled retina.

    What has not been done?
    novelties and techniques
    intentions and inventions,
    styles and modular models compiling:
    a museum of collections – recalled –
    dulls a once determined will.

Still...

    What has been postulated,
    said, dated or postdated
    sung or disclaimed,
    proclaimed over voices' centuries
    does not need re-statement
    or phrase; echoes and rhythms
    not withstanding, all bind to bound:
    paralyzed control is the toll.

With aging, the artist-poet stoops
forced to the corner of consensus:
self equals search, stooped and quiet,
cultures' centuries spun and stopped;
flooded words and sights' memory
overwhelm the consensus of shadows.

The artist-poet, hunched, sits, still
shadow-less and quiet...

The Poem

A thought no longer wished alone
but turning with desire, the yearning
to the beyond what is: and higher:
a reach, a tentative grasp at the gestating wish,
an approach to the beyond behind the comprehensible jest:
the elusive incubating thought made manifest:
the musical complexity of a symphony, expressed –
interwoven thoughts, pauses and paces
appearing, interweaving and disappearing traces
of theme and complexity,
awakened and re-awakened – stressed:
variations, simplifications, complications, a blend, a mix
where all is fixed to rhythms and themes resolved;
words and thoughts that grasp, please and phrase,
rhyme and repeat beyond the ethereal beat, a phase
of weave to recreate the vivid dreams,
the themes of memories that haunt the self alone:
the poem – the seeking to form, to recreate,
to transform the incomprehensible into enduring thought,
the essence of wishing into being from naught:
the forming of a possibility, the beauty of unity
beyond self:
the emotive seeing of being.

Veneto Memory

Passing memories segue –
statues, ghosts and recriminations:
I was there, before
in this Verona square
under the strong sun,
in another time, another August,
and a different person – me.
I – we – I watched
as the children strolled
laughing and licking "gelato",
ice-cream in cups
or colors piled on cones.
Today the square is bare,
empty, except for me
standing here under an archway,
without a shadow, at the fringe,
trying to remember events
and friends, persons,
upon whom memories hinge:
statues, shadows and stones, ghosts,
the statues still stand
golden marble, tinged, to represent,
to replace those gone, displaced,
self abandoned or by time
and times' debilitating strife;
and my life, more empty
stares in at the square
depth and loss
buildings and columns and statues;
but there is no one – no me – there.
A few steps from the shadows,

haltingly, and into the sun:
time is, has again begun:
the statues' shadows slow move,
a minds slow search and pace,
a life elapsed, lost, replaced
with barely a groove or trace;
my self-determined footfalls touch,
there, but without an echo;
no childhood calls
in or from the still silent time;
the sun drenched square dissolves
faltering recollections,
Veneto memory falls.

Once dominating, Dante

Once dominating, divine Dante,
pensive statue in a Verona square,
memories fading
time dissolving
distinct images – vanished,
lost in a confused thought:
only that there was –
once –
a statue, a person, a poet:
friends hiding in Verona
centuries ago;
dementia;
memories lost in the curlicues
and membranes,
pathways and trace ways
of time's exchange – ganglia
and syntax degenerating;
time dissolving
disintegrating memory:
disconnected,
Dante...
Dis- remembered.

Aged

One ages: suddenly
is aged!
Surprise!
Muscles ache, sudden proof
disputes self's lies:
sharp pains
at the bend of a knee,
perception
imperceptibility
imperceptibly
over years –
suddenly, aged:
body disputing mind.

Despite past hints,
suggestions,
time's warnings,
unrecognized tinges:
a wedding rings
sudden uncomfortable fit,
metal's gold –
mental alloy dulls;
mental knowledge
not really believed,
the parties and celebrations
that one is – lulls;
all deceive!...

In spite, despite
contrite, contrary,
then...until the day
an askance glance
passing a store front window,
a humble mirror's
sudden distorted betrayal,
distorted, contorted image –
broken;
dislocated shadows crumble:
past acknowledged;
or the right leg's refusal
to lift
to follow routine,
to jog a neighborhood hill –
collapsed –
a refutation of will;
or the coffee cup,
inexplicably dropped,
dark dull brown stains;
only then
the physical knowledge,
the spreading pain
acknowledged.

The Betrayal,

the separation
between body and mind
body and mind
where once there was one:
now two almost distinct selves
dispute their aspect of being;
the harmony lost,
the automatic ceases,
desists, resists,
falls, collapses
to awareness,
the recognition,
a loss of integration
of unity.
The body no longer obeys
the mind,
the mind the body;
two entities
separated within one;
no reconciliation
to pass from "do"
to "done"...

Inevitable efforts intervene
and succeed
or fail,
the mind's demands,
the body's travail;
fingers swell,
a hand-grip rebels;
mind and body
in the slow, inevitable,
separation,
growth's seeming stasis is broken;
body chemistry's degeneration,
blood numbers confuse – mix,
no balance,
no medical-pharmaceutical fix;
no pills, no reversal;
no jogs up the hill:
futile, refused,
fore – warned is warned:
youth dissipated,
dulling age is age,
a final turn
of the final page.

Shadows' Shades

Nuances
where shadows have shadows,
memories' shades,
and shades have shadows:
haunts and flickers
hints
repeating repetitions,
smoldering intangibles –
obscuring-
accumulating
with the passing hours;
a clock's tick,
pulse paces to thoughts,
traces to time,
memories,
redundancies,
obscuring nuances
of sounds…

Nuances
interiors obsessive
hints, doubts-
semi-thoughts consume
a semi-self:
memories,
that is
what age is,
to be forgotten,
forgetting
the merely years;
what was once,

what was done
or un-done,
histories of memories
or hysterical
colored visions,
attempts, and yearnings
which almost touched,
faltered,
failed;
signs and signals,
sounds,
attachments or more
or worse,
memories forgotten ,
ignored...

A demi-nuanced
a cycle of self
amidst the selfs,
among the non-concerns
almost concerned,
contacts missed, lost
among the disappearing selfs,
self-crowd
concerned with self-
self assumed ,
self un-assumed,
self un-assured,
sureness consumed
in Dante's lowest circle,
memories, shadows and shades...

There-here-
is only the circle,
the one circle left

in which we would preen:
we cycle
shadows barely touched,
attempts,
dissolved wishes,
demi-nuances
not recognizing the shadows,
the shades;
we would walk the conceit
of self, indulged,
confused without indulgences,
abandoned
to that last circle
where shadows have memories,
the memories, shadows,
hints of remnants,
touches of reminders,
traces
of smoldering ash–
a vagueness of a barely
"Once Upon A Time."

Penumbra

Constellations, Galaxies
and the pull of Black Matter:

Universes and Galaxies, and within
time and space trace the personal,
the inevitable of diminishing place,
an individual life damping down: foreclosing…
Outside, as if to deride self,
a full moon and shooting stars:
below, a house reduced to a restricted home,
a face diminished to a personal – "alone!"

Observing science – astronomy – expands,
tracing distinguished webs of matter
in intricate laces, patterns of light
and webs of a fine wrought firmament
bright with promise, intriguing;
the observed star-scattered sky promises,
in spite of the dark unseen,
the controlling, suspected, dark matter.

Subjected, subjective personal place
and time, encompassed, slowly closes:
unseen walls, subtly, previously set,
pinch, are felt, a tightening belt
which constricts health, chance,
constrains choice and opportunity;
the promise of youth is dissolved,
foresworn, and within, beneath breath
blocked, strength and strivings betray,

fortuitous times' offerings slowly decay:
personal self is squeezed endeavor,
diminished, future forcibly trimmed;
"No more storage space
or place in the basement."
The universe expands, galaxies splay:
life's unheard din derides a self
self whimpering, reduced to whim.

In the Desert

In the desert
beneath the arches
and before the stones,
storms and tenuous approach
acknowledge the presence,
the essence,
of memories retracing repetitions,
visions of time
across time:
the two men bend
and genuflect:
a blend of wind blown distances
before the bent knee;
before the incantations,
their thoughts reach
to the rocks – the spirit –
to sand and yet not sand,
impervious, impermanence,
songs and prayers seeking,
searching the spiritual:
seen, imagined,
dry desert illusions
amidst a flood of images,
wind touched and aged rocks,
ochre-white clouds, and grey,
all suggestions, memories,
mirrors of times to come:
departed spirits' songs
and past
reflect and are sung,
hung on vapors of air,

ethereal images
ochre-grey clouds
and dirt devils, blown :
remembrance
without answer…

Terminal/Transition

Star struck infatuated youth
unanswered
generations asked, unrealized;
would it have mattered,
made a difference
when I had married – first –
once, generations, scores ago?
Tattered youth doesn't know,
only hypothesis and hopes
without understanding,
implications too easily misread:
the destination is the going,
the stop is involuntary,
validating or not…
unforeseen, unnoticed, the bump
in the hill, the hump of diversion,
the divergence,
bend, break of the road,
the parting and the stop,
the division of intent,
self interest
and the ambulatory of way…
repetition; transition:
youth- one
can never be correct
or answered:
to go is not to know
where the splitting starts
or the going ends….

Re-dux

Silk Threads

He couldn't keep up the flight
the emotional soaring
the aspiration, the inspiration-
the lift- the light
promise of altitude
attitude and unspoken thought:
suggested aspirations
and delicate motions,
gentle devotions, a quiet touch,
a floating
that barely breathed.

How much could they,
she, he expect?
Gentleness and want
desire and concern-
a filament-
a fulfillment of promise?

High school youth-
a suggestive smile,
a mentality carried forward
to times future warp;
the web spun
the thread
of always still seventeen,
always future to come
promise to be:
wistful wishing,
tempting, reaching , searing
acting and reacting...

I hold my breath
expecting the heartache
of youth - and you –
unfulfilled:
silk filament,
Gone!

Better a Baked Blueberry

One Does what one is,
One Is what one Does:

What one does, one Is;
What one Is
determines what one Is
and to Become:

Before the window
watching
within an isolation
of the self,
in the city
in the house
in the blue music room
with the blue window
with the blue shadows
amidst the notes
and musical runs,
blue ruins,
the internal confusions,
audible locutions
and self defeated resolutions,
the rhythmic isolation,
the contemplation-
the perpetuation
of the alone-
of the shards
of the shattered self :

Music overwhelms a silence.

One is, one does
together-
alone with the self,
the conflicted self;
the remnants of a figure,
a man broken in the blue window,
reflected and repeated,
shattered experiment in paint
and shuttered print
and mumbled words:

self is a work created
in the image of self
untracked
unframed
un-noticed,
dislocated,
to be hung-
or cellar-stored,
unseen
within the isolation
of the fragile self.

What one does, one Is;
What one is, one does:
One Is, reflecting shards
stored in ignored isolation...

I can't hold the image,
retain the self,
the reflections,
the mental pictures
of the blurred, shattered
blue window

anymore:
fading, falling
born to be still born,
I can't hold the images
the slippery mental pictures
distorting,
the hazy blue window
image shredding, shedding
self bits any longer…

Anymore.

If there is someone-
anyone- out there-
somewhere- Please-
pass in
a blue berry sherbet .

City Vendors

City flowers
and silk filaments,
blossoms and threads,
green stalks growing
amidst bright yellows,
color showers
amidst purple reds:
floral combinations,
alternations,
alliterations,
weaving and woven,
fantasy in tapestry
from tended gardens,
brick-red walls,
low grey-cement divisions
and wooden stalls:
visions from divisions
tapestries and murals...

City flowers,
sidewalk sellers,
street-side hawking,
implications,
alliterations:
brown man, white man,
poor men hustling,
bustling
for the weekend stash:
city grown roses,
fresh flowers for sale,
curbside vendors

pressing for their weekend stash:
" flowers for a lady friend"
a smile, a hope
for a bit of cash

City gardens
attended,
intended
city grown dreams;
manicured lots
and rented spaces,
cultivated hopes
belie anxious faces:
city flowers
and silk filaments,
blossoms and threads
created, worked
bright yellows and greens
amidst the purples and reds…

City vendors:
Plant a garden
Toss a bouquet !